Everything is bullshit

rachel scott

Presentation by *BookLeaf Publishing*

Web: www.bookleafpub.com

E-mail: info@bookleafpub.com

ISBN: 9789357744270

First edition 2023

Kids toys adult issues

When I was 10, my cousins and I loaded up a McDonald's mini backpack with a plastic canteen of water and plastic food (no clue why), and set off to make it in the "wilderness"
 The wilderness to us was the plot of land behind their house that was about to be developed with mounds of dirt dug up, grass high as our shoulders and a scorching Texas sun.
 We walked what seemed like miles on our journey through the wilderness with nothing but walkie talkies, a plastic canteen, McDonald's lunch pail and excitement. We were conquering a mission that felt bestowed upon us, so holy that it wasn't even discussed before hand.
 We walked and walked, and by the time we were done, the walkie talkies were glued to our hands, the canteen became a flask, and our innocence was gone

The Ocean has red tape

They will section off plots of land on mars
 Next they will divide the ocean with red tape
 Everything is on sale, color, letter, tree,
 Every part of life that you didn't think could be
dissected and bought will be
 And then we will have nothing left
 No greenery to run to for escape
 Only concrete and technology
 And it will be okay because we will be busy
 So, so busy with our token economy

The war of art

Art is for the fighters
 It is the soul pulling out that which the mind
does not know
 It is the war within your spirit splattered on a
blank canvas like a bleeding heart
 It is your desperation, your happiness, your rage
 Coming together to form a treaty of peace
 Between the duality inside of you

The state of Journalism

The tv is full of negative news
 Sensational news which only considers views
 Meanwhile; the news most important is what
they choose to ruse
 Confuse us they may but we will recuse
 Journalists, where is the truth you say you
value?
 Has anyone asked the purpose of the news?
 People basked in fear are easier to control and
move
 For one day the truth will come out ; billionaire
owners of the news and the government
certainty shmooze
 Plotting for power and more revenue
 They certainly do

All the little things

All your habits add up, so be careful what you
choose
The smallest things we take for granted
Breathing, Speaking, Seeing
And where you place your value

It's a subtle, beautiful part of life because all
your decisions build
Are you the person you want to be?
All the little things matter, what you do, say and
think
I want you to have life more fulfilled ♥

Insta-worthy

Am I sufficiently beautiful?
To look like all the other girls on instagram?
To be adequately useable?

To marry quickly to a giant tool?
To look down on others with proud ridicule?
Am I sufficiently beautiful?

To fraternize with only the shallow suitable?
To have the same Botox face as every other
vestibule?
To be adequately useable?

To become doable?
With my giant fake ass that might kill me
Am I sufficiently beautiful?

To have a lack of depth as usual?
Does my face lack enough age and emotion?
To be adequately useable?

Am I beautiful enough
To be adequately usable?

A limerick

The government: a show of grandeur
 Two parties with co-stars voyeur
 We pay their bills
 And they shovel us pills
 To pretend we are in the matrix no more

Progress

The beauty is vast
However polluted by
Our need to control

Enigma Sunset

The pinks and blues clouded my eyes when I was on the sacred plant much like the sunsets I have always loved
 They were your favorite colors too and deepened the mystery
 The fluffy little clouds that we listened to in the sun, the sand contrast to ocean so limitless and eternal; as the gradients of color run deep and expansive like my range of emotions
 But it is in my same-ness that I am still an enigma, just like you; just like the pink and blue sunsets that followed me from my childhood to our friendship with undefined hues
 The pinks and blues that remind me of you will always be my halcyon but like a Pantone I now match my life to a more diverse range of colors
 The pinks and blues clouded my eyes when I was on the sacred plant but I saw you; naked, laughing, crying, and the sun is still shining on us, still creating pinks and blues

Aesthetics

Body dysmorphic disorder
 The physical embodiment of perfectionism
 She admits she has it in her instagram caption;
 Her face full of make-up and filler
 A sacrifice for the algorithm
 People still comment to admire how beautiful
she is
 I appreciate the kindness; however what is the
message behind this?

 If we are only paying attention to the beauty, we
may miss the underlying meaning (thanks Daria)

 It's interesting how people do things that make
them look good- the perfect spouse, perfect
house, perfectly curated social media image
 Isn't it funny how the face that looks good on
instagram doesn't look as good in reality?

 People say they just want to be happy
 Is your soul happy or are you putting on a show
for ego?

 Isn't it strange how we aren't accomplished
unless everyone else knows we did it?

Sometimes the most aesthetically beautiful people are just empty fake faces with deceptive visage

Is God SpongeBob?

Call it the universe or
 You can call it god
 Or even SpongeBob
 But something is listening

ver·i·si·mil·i·tude

Watch those sneaky journalists! They are merely consigned
 A subtle word, here and there that imprints in your mind
 An idea that gets woven into the fabric of society
 One that as more and more people internalize, seems right, full of propriety

 Watch the preachers! They act lofty on piety; they have convinced even themselves that they have all the answers
 Glorified financiers
 Society! Stop giving them notoriety!
 The money they take for their megachurch puts them high atop their yacht
 Who knew that salvation could be bought

 Watch for political extremists! So certain of their correctness
 We all want answers
 Thinking you are wholly right is only reckless
 It is when you realize you are in a bubble that you are set free
 They profit off of the class struggle

Brainwashing is subtle
There is a reason words like verisimilitude
came to be

I know who you are

You smile to me
But inside you are judging
I will judge you too //

Your smile is genuine
I am still afraid
There is much a smile holds

God in a box

Does God exist by some arbitrary rules that your
(insert here) people made up?
 He's Jew ! He's Christian!
 He's angry! He's compassionate!
 He's nothing! There is no god!
 If you follow these rules that we made up, you
go to heaven!
 If you follow this narcissists content, you'll
know what heaven is!
 Come with me, I know all the answers
 (He says God spoke to him-send him some
money)
 Meanwhile, God looks down on us, puzzling at
our futile attempts to explain what we are not
meant to
 God is It; It that which we don't know what It is
 God is not caught; it is sand sifting through our
hands

Words are powerful

What sets us apart from the other living beings?
 We have the ability to speak
 We have the ability to create things
 And we take it for granted
 There is an element of magic
 In our world,
 That even the trained eye cannot see
 If you're mindful, you can feel it all around
you, even at most candid

Shallow

You only exist if you have a highlight reel
 With the tv make up
 And with it a "reality" show to go
 See how good I look!

 You're only a friend if you make me look
important
 With the right type of everything
 And a head filled with nothing
 See how good we look!

 Youre only a friend if you can do something for
me
 But not help me grow as a person
 You see
 I already look my best version !

Career woman

We will do the dance where I tell you how bad I
want to work here for piss poor wages
 I will show nothing but glee
 You will tell me annually there is a 50cent raise
 I will pretend my boss doesn't sexually harass
me
 Or if she's a woman; act fake and catty

 More metrics! More money! More measurables!
 Society calls people lazy if they don't pretend
this is pleasurable

 While entertainers make millions to distract us
from the truth
 Appeasing us like a glass of vermouth
 And meanwhile we ride, ride, ride on stationary
bikes

 The definition of work; it's time to change our
reasons!
 What brings people joy? Genuine connection
and freedom
 It's time for a new season

Agency

If everything is bullshit, are we screwed?
 Whats the point of anything?
 It's easy to believe there's nothing more, of course,
 and that you have no power here,
 but you actually do

 Spend time in quiet, in calm
 Spend time reading, creating, questioning, nurturing, awaiting
 Reset your nervous system
 Don't allow the chaos to shake you

 Ask your soul what's best for you to do,
 What is the loving thing, but also the truest path for you?

 They deceive, saying you only have one life!
But what if there's more?
 That is the trick you see,
 Take agency!
 Don't allow your purpose to be robbed by complacency!

The cost of narcissism

I must be more than basic !
 Parties with only pretty faces!
I really want to be special
Only associate with High level !
I want my name to be known !
Anything to make me feel proven!

I deserve to be around wealthy people!
And take what I can get!
Dispose of you when I'm done as if you are
fecal!
Social climb to get my selfish desires met
All the tangible solutions!

The rest are obsessed until they conceive
It's all smoke and mirrors
So many living to look superior
With nothing underneath the illusion

 Superiority and inferiority are two sides of the
same token
 Both hold separation, desperation and
unhappiness
 Let them live in their state of delusion

Highs and lows

I traveled the cities in convertibles and
rollerskates
 I did a lot of fun things and went on plenty of
dates

 I went through a depression as dark as the sky
 So physically and mentally sick I didn't think
I'd survive

 I lived a life of extremes, it was time to have
some calm
 I worked through my trauma and read a lot of
psalms

 I lived in a jungle, I went through it all
 I thank God for opening my eyes
 All these experiences made me wise
 I prayed the whole time, God didn't let me fall

Everything is bullshit

Everything may be bullshit
 But it's also beautiful
 Existence can be drab
 But it's also meaningful
 Everyone sucks
 But there's kindness all around
 You will meet eyes with someone very
profound
 Everything may be bullshit
 But it's also beautiful
 You see, there's two sides to everything
 One side carol baskin, one side tiger king
 And if we analyze the side we are worshipping
 We just might see the beauty in everything
 Everything is still beautiful

www.ingramcontent.com/pod-product-compliance
Lightning Source LLC
LaVergne TN
LVHW050306200726
843509LV00015B/3181